Finding Peace Amidst the Noise: Embracing Stillness

JOHN M. LOPEZ

INTRODUCTION: The Quest for Inner Peace

In an ever-changing world, the desire of inner serenity is a timeless endeavor that transcends cultural, regional, and individual barriers. It is a quest for a profound sense of calm that comes from inside, a quiet that helps us to face life's obstacles with serenity and grace. The longing for inner peace stems from a fundamental human drive to find consolation, balance, and meaning in a quickly changing and sometimes chaotic existence.

Inner calm is not a passive state of being; it is an active and intentional journey that demands self-awareness, introspection, and a willingness to confront one's own mind's intricacies. It entails recognizing the whirlwind of ideas, emotions, and external stimuli that compete for our attention all the time. The quest for inner calm begins with acknowledging that our inner environment is frequently as turbulent as the world outside. This awareness lays the groundwork for the development of mindfulness and presence, both of which are necessary skills in the search of serenity.

The route to inner calm sometimes necessitates redefining our connection with external circumstances. It entails learning to separate oneself from outcomes over which we have no control and finding peace in the midst of uncertainty. This does not imply ignoring the world's problems, but rather acquiring the ability to respond rather than react. It is about recognizing our ability to select our ideas, feelings, and behaviors regardless of the circumstances.

Meditation, deep breathing, and awareness become helpful partners on the path to inner calm. These techniques provide us skills to help us focus our attention in the present moment, gently shoving aside the continual mental chatter that adds to our restlessness. We learn to watch our thoughts without judgment via these practices, gradually untangling ourselves from their grasp and enabling a place for stillness to arise.

The pursuit of inner peace also entails letting go – letting go of ties to the past, worries about the future, and the constant desire for external validation. This approach allows us to make place for acceptance and thankfulness. Acceptance does not indicate resignation; rather, it means accepting life as it is, with all of its flaws. Gratitude, on the other hand, assists us in shifting our emphasis from what is lacking to what we already have, cultivating a sense of contentment that is independent of external circumstances.

Perhaps the most important component of the quest for inner peace is the knowledge that it is a journey rather than a destination. It's a path that necessitates patience, self-compassion, and a dedication to personal development. Inner serenity is preserved by an unflinching willingness to meet hardships head on, learn from them, and progress as a consequence, much as a river runs despite impediments.

In a culture that values perpetual activity and external accomplishment, seeking inner serenity may appear contradictory. However, it is a knowledge that true fulfillment comes from a profound sense of inner contentment rather than external praise. The pursuit of inner peace is not an escape from reality; rather, it is a bold and deliberate engagement with reality. It's a voyage that asks us to go into the depths of our own being in order to discover the wellspring of knowledge and resilience that exists inside us.

As we begin on this journey, we realize that inner serenity is not an elusive ideal reserved for the spiritually enlightened. It is a birthright, available to everybody prepared to begin on the road of self-discovery. The pursuit of inner peace is an invitation to befriend ourselves, to find consolation in our own company, and to construct an inner refuge where calm prevails in the midst of worldly cacophony. It is a path that not only provides personal growth but also the opportunity to contribute to a more peaceful and harmonious world.

PART I: UNDERSTANDING THE ESSENCE OF STILLNESS

CHAPTER 1. Defining Stillness: Beyond Silence and Inaction

Stillness, which is sometimes misunderstood as the lack of movement or sound, is a condition of tremendous depth and richness that stretches well beyond quiet and immobility. It's a concept that extends beyond the physical world, into the realms of the mind, emotions, and even the spiritual. To characterize stillness as a lack of movement is to ignore its nuanced and transforming nature, which has the capacity to anchor us in the present moment and provide a break from life's never-ending tumult.

Silence, which is generally linked with the lack of noise, is only one aspect of stillness. Stillness entails a stillness that is not confined to exterior auditory sensations; it is an inner silence that may be created in the midst of a chaotic orchestra of ideas, emotions, and external stimuli. This inner stillness is not a blank, but rather a place for the mind to rest and for clarity and insight to develop. Thoughts may develop and pass in this state, but they no longer dominate our attention; they are like clouds drifting over the sky of our consciousness.

Equally crucial is the realization that quiet does not imply inactivity. It's not about getting apathetic or disconnected from the world. It is, instead, an active condition of being that enables intentional interaction with the present moment. When we remain genuinely still, we are entirely present with whatever we are doing, whether it is enjoying a cup of tea, conversing, or working on a creative project. This aware presence gives our activities depth and significance, converting mundane duties into moments of grace and meaning.

Stillness has a deeper meaning in the area of emotions that goes beyond the mind and actions. It is not a place where emotions are suppressed, but rather a place where they may be felt and recognized without being swept away by their intensity. Stillness is a refuge in the middle of life's storms, allowing us to examine our emotional currents, gaining insight into their origins and allowing them to gradually decrease. This emotional stillness is not detachment, but a caring presence that promotes self-awareness and emotional equilibrium.

Furthermore, the spiritual aspect of quiet invites us to connect with something bigger than ourselves. It's a place where we can find oneness, transcendence, and inner wisdom. As a method of enhancing this connection, many spiritual traditions employ activities that encourage quiet. Individuals attempt to touch the calm that exists at the heart of their being, connecting with a source of serenity that goes beyond the boundaries of the material world, whether via prayer, meditation, or contemplative activities.

In a culture that glorifies perpetual movement and commotion, the skill of embracing silence is a paradoxical but necessary pursuit. It asks us to abandon the continuous chase of outward successes in order to explore the riches of our inner world. It's an invitation to delve into the intricacies of presence, the textures of stillness, and the expansiveness of the mind. We learn from this investigation that silence is a process of constant refining and discovery, rather than a destination.

To define stillness as the absence of movement or sound is to only touch the surface of its possibilities. True stillness is a broad condition that includes the mind, heart, and soul. It's a voyage that takes us beyond the surface and into the profound, where we may discover the beauty and peace that exist inside us, ready to be welcomed among life's never-ending currents.

CHAPTER 2. The Science of Serenity: How Stillness Impacts the Mind and Body

Scientific study is illuminating the nuanced ways in which cultivating silence may lead to greater well-being, stress reduction, and cognitive performance. This increasing knowledge of serenity science is providing light on how silence may be used as a great tool for holistic health.

Stillness Neurobiology: Restoring Balance
Neuroscientific research has revealed that practicing stillness, particularly mindfulness meditation, can result in anatomical and functional changes in the brain. Meditation on a regular basis has been linked to increased gray matter density in brain areas associated with emotional control, attention, and self-awareness. These changes are associated with increased emotional resilience and decreased response to stresses.

Furthermore, during moments of deep quiet, the brain's default mode network (DMN), which is responsible for self-referential thinking and mind-wandering, becomes less active. This decrease in DMN activity has been linked to greater sensations of present-moment awareness and less rumination, resulting in a calmer and more focused mind.

The Relaxation Response and Stress Reduction

One of the most well-documented impacts of stillness is its potential to elicit the relaxation response, which is characterized by a slower heart rate, lower blood pressure, and lower levels of stress chemicals such as cortisol. When the body enters this condition, it suppresses the "fight or flight" reaction that prolonged stress may cause, allowing for physical and mental regeneration.

Individuals who participate in activities such as meditation, deep breathing, and progressive muscle relaxation enjoy not just instant relaxation but also long-term advantages in stress management, according to research. Slowing down and cultivating quiet purposely engages the parasympathetic nerve system, which promotes relaxation, digestion, and repair inside the body.

Cognitive Enhancements: Mind Sharpening
Contrary to popular belief, stillness does not result in mental stagnation. Instead, evidence shows that cultivating stillness might improve cognitive performance. Meditation, for example, has been related to improved attention, memory, and cognitive flexibility. Regular practitioners frequently demonstrate improved capacity to maintain concentration, transition between activities, and resist distractions.

Another important part of the science of tranquility is neuroplasticity, or the brain's ability to reshape itself in response to events. Activities that encourage quiet can help to develop brain networks related to self-regulation, emotional processing, and executive functioning. This suggests that people who practice stillness on a regular basis may find it easier to regulate their emotions, make sensible judgments, and handle difficult circumstances over time.

Sleep and Rest: Embracing the Stillness of the Night

The influence of quiet extends to sleep, where restorative sleep is essential for general well-being. Sleep problems and poor sleep quality are frequently associated with increased stress and anxiety. Relaxation and mindfulness activities before bedtime can generate a sense of peace and tranquility, easing the transition into deep, restful sleep.

Sleep becomes more peaceful and restorative when the mind is calm and free of rushing thoughts. By minimizing the mental chatter that might keep people awake at night, stillness helps to establish an atmosphere favorable to better sleep hygiene. As a result, the science of tranquility has gone full circle, providing advantages that extend from the domain of waking moments to the realm of dreams.

In a culture that typically prizes perpetual activity and noise, the new science of tranquility emphasizes the real advantages of cultivating silence. Scientific study is increasingly recognizing the effects of quiet on the mind and body, from neurobiological alterations to stress reduction and cognitive benefits. Mindfulness meditation, deep breathing, and progressive relaxation, for example, can lead to higher emotional well-being, better stress management, improved cognitive performance, and more restful sleep. Individuals may use the power of quiet to negotiate the complexity of modern life with more comfort and resilience by knowing and embracing the science of tranquility.

PART II: EMBRACING STILLNESS IN DAILY LIFE

CHAPTER 3. Stillness In Action: Integrating Tranquility into Your Routine

Stillness may appear incongruous with the concept of activity in a world that lives on perpetual movement and demands. However, incorporating serenity into your everyday routine, sometimes known as "stillness in action," provides a transforming method to negotiate life's obstacles with increased clarity, awareness, and efficacy. This method acknowledges that stillness is not an antithesis to motion, but rather a necessary component that may improve the quality of your interactions with the environment.

Accepting Mindful Presence

The notion of conscious presence is at the heart of stillness in action. Stillness allows you to engage in each action with complete concentration and awareness, rather than hurrying through things on autopilot. Whether you're doing the dishes, answering emails, or commuting, approaching these tasks attentively may transform your experience from one of rush to one of awareness.

Immersing oneself entirely in the activity at hand entails examining your thoughts and experiences without judgment. This technique not only improves your enjoyment of the current moment, but it also lowers stress and improves the quality of your activities. When you bring calmness to your actions, each work may emerge with purpose and meaning.

Making Space for Silence
Adopting a monastic lifestyle is not required to include calm into your everyday. It's about incorporating moments of quiet throughout your day, even when things are hectic. These are

quick yet powerful moments. Taking a few deep breaths before a meeting, walking outdoors to admire nature during a break, or just pausing to taste a drink of tea can all serve as mini-retreats that give relief from the rush may all function as mini-retreats that provide respite from the rush.

These quiet intervals serve as reset buttons for the mind, enabling you to refresh and concentrate. They remind you that you may find peace in the middle of chaos, fostering your inner well-being even when the outside world is chaotic.

Developing Mindful Transitions
Transitions are excellent times to develop stillness in action. Intermissions between work, meetings, or activities can be used to take a few focused breaths or practice a quick centering meditation. You take the peace of quiet with you by intentionally shifting from one task to the next, cultivating a smooth flow between times of action and periods of contemplation.

17

Mindful transitions can also help to keep mental clutter at bay. When you bring quiet to these transitional periods, you lessen your chances of carrying extra tension or distractions from one activity to the next. This not only improves your efficiency, but it also keeps you calm and focused.

Stillness promotes efficiency.
Contrary to popular opinion, including serenity into your daily routine might actually increase your productivity. When you approach activities with a clear and peaceful mind, your decisions become more deliberate, and your actions become more meaningful. The discipline of stillness in activity lowers attention dispersion, helping you to better use your mental resources. Furthermore, stillness improves your capacity to prioritize things and manage your time effectively. You may guarantee that your activities are aligned with your genuine priorities by spending a few seconds to center yourself and evaluate your goals. This avoids the temptation

of being engrossed in never-ending activities without making genuine progress.

Stillness in activity is a harmonic synthesis of awareness and involvement. It does not demand you to quit your obligations or seek seclusion; rather, it encourages you to bring a sense of calm to every situation. You may improve your general well-being, reduce stress, and approach your everyday chores with better clarity and intention by practicing mindful presence, establishing moments of silence, and fostering mindful transitions.

Integrating serenity into your daily routine elevates your actions from ordinary chores to meaningful experiences. You may cultivate a balanced and purposeful way of life by bridging the gap between the demands of the exterior world and the calm of your inner world through silence. Finally, stillness in action provides a means of negotiating the difficulties of modern life with grace, awareness, and a profound feeling of connectedness to the present moment.

CHAPTER 4. Mindful Moments: Cultivating Presence through Stillness

In a society filled with continual distractions and a relentless pace, establishing attentive moments provides a powerful antidote. These mindfulness-infused moments of silence give a respite from the turmoil and a portal to a deeper connection with the present moment. Individuals may modify their experience of life, improve their well-being, and cultivate a feeling of balance in the face of life's pressures by consciously generating and cultivating these pockets of presence.

The Influence of Mindful Presence
The act of being completely involved in the present moment, without judgment or distraction, is known as mindful presence. It entails paying conscious attention to the sensations, ideas, and emotions that occur in each instant. You have a heightened awareness of your experiences as a result, allowing you to participate with life more truly and fully.

It's easy to get caught up in automatic routines and habitual reflexes in the midst of daily life. This autopilot state is interrupted by mindful moments, which invite you to break free from the cycle of response and enter the domain of conscious decision. When you inject attentive present into your actions and conversations, you transform each event from a routine chore to a meaningful encounter.

Making Mindful Environments

Mindful moments can occur in a variety of contexts and situations. They do not need a certain environment or time; rather, they are concerned with purpose and attention. You may create thoughtful spaces in your day by pausing before entering a meeting to take a few deep breaths, or by consciously tasting the tastes of your food. These small pauses help you to transition from "doing" mode to "being" mode, centering yourself in the present moment and connecting with your inner experience.

Nature may also be a great place to cultivate thoughtful moments. A stroll in a park, a trek in the woods, or simply gazing at a peaceful scene may all help you feel more present. Nature's beauty naturally encourages calm, and engaging with it consciously allows you to connect with the world around you on a deeper level.

Making Routine a Ritual

Routine actions may be transformed into meaningful rituals by including conscious presence. Brushing your teeth, washing your hands, and even folding laundry may all become moments for mindfulness. Bring your attention to the feelings, textures, and motions while you participate in these exercises. By approaching these routines as contemplative moments, you add depth and intention to your daily life.

Technology and digital gadgets may also be part of mindful routines. Consider bringing awareness into your encounters with technology instead of aimlessly browsing through social media or emails. Pause before checking your phone, take a breath, and then proceed mindfully. This simple gesture can assist you in breaking free from the continual tug of distraction and cultivating a more thoughtful relationship with technology.

Emotional Resilience Development

Mindful moments provide more than simply a break from outside distractions; they also promote emotional resilience. You create a place for your emotions to be noticed and processed by engaging with them thoughtfully. You allow uncomfortable emotions to arise and dissolve naturally, without judgment, rather than repressing or avoiding them.

You may examine your emotions as they arise, note their body sensations, and watch them fade away via attentive present. This activity improves emotional intelligence and prevents unpleasant emotions from escalating. Mindful moments serve as a container for holding your feelings without becoming overwhelmed by them.

Accepting Impermanence

Mindful moments also lead to a greater grasp of life's impermanence. By totally immersing oneself in each experience, you become more aware of how transitory events are. This awareness fosters thankfulness for the current moment as well as a disconnection from the need to cling to or escape events.

When you connect with the world mindfully, you begin to see how life develops moment by moment. This awareness frees you from worrying about the future or regretting the past, allowing you to accept the beauty and significance of the current moment.
Mindful moments serve as stepping stones to a more mindful and fulfilled existence. By generating and fostering these moments of silence and presence on purpose, you add depth, significance, and awareness to your experiences. The discipline of generating mindful moments does not need a lot of time or complicated strategies; it just involves paying complete attention to whatever you are doing.

In a culture that frequently emphasizes multitasking and continual stimulation, thoughtful moments provide a counterbalance—a way to find sanctuary amid the turmoil. Connecting with the present moment via mindful presence gives you the opportunity to experience life more completely, truthfully, and gratefully for each passing moment. You open the door to a more conscious and enriched way of being by fostering attentive moments.

PART III: OVERCOMING CHALLENGES ON THE PATH TO STILLNESS

CHAPTER 5. Taming the Monkey Mind: Quieting Inner Restlessness

Within the depths of our awareness exists a phenomena known as the "monkey mind." This phrase aptly describes the restless, noisy, and frequently surprising character of our thoughts. The monkey mind jumps from branch to branch, juggling anxieties, regrets, plans, and distractions. Finding peace and tranquility in the middle of this mental tumult can be difficult. It is, nevertheless, possible to tame the monkey mind and build a more tranquil and focused mental landscape via practice and mindfulness.

Recognizing the Monkey Mind

The monkey mind is a metaphor describing the mind's proclivity to leap from idea to concept, much like a monkey. It's the never-ending internal story, the mental chatter that might accompany us from the time we wake up until the moment we fall asleep. This continual stream of ideas can cause inner restlessness, making truly engaging with the present moment challenging.

Replaying previous experiences, worrying about the future, analyzing, evaluating, and even engaging in negative self-talk are all examples of how the monkey mind manifests itself. It thrives on ambiguity and attempts to assert control over events outside our immediate control. This inner instability not only generates worry and anxiety, but it also inhibits us from enjoying true serenity and well-being.

The Advantages of Taming the Monkey Mind
Taming the monkey mind and cultivating calm inside the mind can result in a variety of advantages for mental and emotional well-being. By clearing out mental clutter, you make room for clarity, attention, and creativity. Quieting the monkey mind helps you to face situations with

greater serenity, make more informed judgments, and enjoy a deeper sense of happiness.

Taming the monkey mind also improves emotional management. When your mind isn't continuously being pushed in multiple ways, you're better able to respond to emotions in a balanced manner. You can perceive and accept your feelings without being overwhelmed by their intensity, which is essential for emotional well-being.

Techniques for Taming the Monkey Mind
Taming the monkey mind is a long-term process that requires perseverance and regular effort. Various mindfulness and meditation activities can assist you in training your mind to calm and find quiet in the midst of chaos:

1. Mindful Awareness: Mindfulness entails monitoring your thoughts without passing judgment on them. Rather than becoming engrossed in the substance of your thoughts, practice detached awareness. like ideas come,

notice them and allow them to pass, just like clouds do in the sky.

2.   Focused   Attention   Meditation: In   this technique,   you   devote   your   attention   to   an anchor, such as your breath or a specific sound. When your thoughts begin to stray, gently draw your attention back to the chosen anchor. This improves   your   capacity   to   stay   present   over time.

3. Body Scan Meditation: Bring your focus to different regions of your body, beginning with your toes and working your way up to your head. This exercise allows you to connect with your bodily sensations, grounding you in the present moment and distracting your mind from its ramblings.

4. Journaling: Writing down your ideas and feelings might aid in the externalization of mental chatter. Giving your ideas a physical form allows you to acquire perspective and a sense of relief.

5. Walking Meditation: Practice mindful walking by paying attention to the sensation of each step, your breath, and the surroundings. This practice blends movement and mindfulness to provide a dynamic method of mind-stilling.

Developing Patience and Kindness

Patience and self-compassion are required for taming the monkey mind. It's critical to understand that the mind's restlessness is a natural phenomena, and the objective isn't to eradicate all ideas. It's more about changing your connection with your thoughts and learning to direct your attention with purpose.

Be kind with yourself throughout this time. It's normal for your mind to fight your attempts. When you sense your attention drifting, gently lead it back to the current moment. With persistent practice, the monkey mind will begin to calm, and moments of silence and clarity will become more accessible.

Taming the monkey mind is an inner change and self-discovery path. You can achieve more clarity, emotional balance, and a deeper connection to the present moment by honing the capacity to calm the restless chatter of the mind. You may progressively educate your mind to discover calm via mindfulness and meditation techniques, allowing you to experience life more fully and truthfully. Remember that the road is just as essential as the destination, and that with each step, you're cultivating inner serenity and well-being.

CHAPTER 6. Letting Go of Attachments: Finding Freedom in Detachment

Attachments are emotional relationships that we develop with people, objects, ideas, and results. While attachments can offer us delight, they can also cause us pain if we grow excessively reliant on them for our happiness and well-being. Letting go of attachments, also known as detachment, is a significant journey toward emotional liberation and spiritual serenity. It entails letting up of expectations, outcomes, and the need for external validation, allowing us to feel a greater feeling of satisfaction and empowerment.

Comprehending Attachments

Attachments develop as a result of our desires and aversions. When we want something or someone, we associate our pleasure and well-being with the fulfillment of that desire. When we have aversions, we avoid particular experiences or outcomes in order to prevent discomfort or pain. When things don't go as planned, these attachments link us to the unpredictability and impermanence of life, causing irritation, worry, and a sense of powerlessness.

Attachments may take many forms, including attachment to relationships, monetary belongings, job success, a certain self-image, or even specific ideas and viewpoints. While having preferences and wishes is acceptable, being overly tied to them can lead to a cycle of pain when reality does not match our expectations.

Detachment as a Concept

Detachment does not imply being apathetic or removed from life. It is not about hiding feelings or dismissing the importance of connections and experiences. Detachment, on the other hand, is a process of developing a healthy connection with our impulses and attachments. It's about holding things gently, acknowledging their impermanence, and finding freedom from their influence.

Detachment entails letting go of the desire for outside conditions to define our inner state of being. It is about establishing an internal center of control in which our well-being is not exclusively dependent on external events. Detachment does not erase want; rather, it changes our relationship to desire, helping us to negotiate life's ups and downs with greater calm.

The Influence of Letting Go
It might be difficult to let go of attachments since they frequently symbolize our goals, dreams, and sense of self. The act of letting go, on the other hand, provides deep release. When we let go of attachments, we make room for acceptance, satisfaction, and personal progress.

By letting go of the demand for precise results, we minimize anxiety and break free from the never-ending cycle of worrying about the future. This does not imply abandoning ambitions or desires; rather, it is approaching them with an open hand and an open heart, allowing for flexibility and adaptability.

Developing Detachment

Cultivating detachment is an ongoing process that requires self-awareness and attention. Here are some steps to help you through the process of letting go:

1. Self-Reflection: Take some time to consider your attachments in your life. Take note of the emotional intensity and how it influences your thoughts and behaviors.

2. Recognize Patterns: Recognize repeated attachment patterns and how they affect your well-being. Is there anything that causes greater attachments or aversions?

3. Develop Mindfulness: Mindfulness helps you to see your attachments without passing judgment on them. This awareness provides a

space between input and response, allowing you to choose how to respond.

4. Practice thankfulness: Develop thankfulness for what you have right now. Attachments can be lessened by focusing on what you have rather than what you need.

5. Accept Impermanence: Consider the impermanence of all things. Accepting that everything changes might make it easier to let go.

6. Meditation: Meditation may aid in the development of mental clarity as well as emotional resilience. Loving-kindness meditation, for example, may promote connection while also increasing separation.

7. Exercise Non-Attachment: Participate in activities without clinging to the results. Approach work, relationships, and experiences with an open heart, knowing that whatever happens will be a learning experience.

The Way of Liberation

Letting go of attachments is a path that leads to freedom from the emotional roller coaster that cravings and aversions create. It leads to a great sense of independence, resilience, and inner serenity. Detachment does not imply abandoning life's beauty and richness; rather, it permits you to enjoy life more completely, totally, and truly.

You develop the ability to embrace life with open arms as you practice detachment, while also recognizing that genuine pleasure is not dependent on external circumstances. You make room for acceptance, happiness, and a higher capacity to respond to life's problems with grace and wisdom when you discover freedom in detachment. Let go eventually leads to a more harmonious connection with yourself, others, and the ever-changing environment around you.

PART IV: PRACTICES AND TECHNIQUES FOR STILLNESS

CHAPTER 7. Meditation Unveiled: Exploring the Depths of Inner Silence

In the midst of modern life's clamor, meditation serves as a refuge—a road to the tranquil depths of inner solitude. Meditation, which is sometimes misunderstood as a lonely practice for monks or spiritual adepts, is, in reality, a universally accessible technique for increasing awareness, lowering stress, and exploring the limitless horizons of the human mind. Meditation, behind its superficial connections, reveals a deep path of self-discovery, providing a transforming experience that resonates across cultures, ages, and walks of life.

The Meaning of Meditation

Meditation is fundamentally about establishing a concentrated and undistracted state of mind. It is not about ridding the mind of thoughts, but rather about learning to watch them without becoming caught in them. You become an observer of your thoughts, emotions, and sensations by sitting quietly and turning your attention within. This technique helps you to get better self-awareness and insight into your mental habits.

Meditation techniques can range from concentrated concentration to open awareness, and from guided visions to loving-kindness exercises. Each approach serves as a distinct entry point to the same goal: the investigation of the inner landscape and the revelation of the depths of inner quiet.

The Inner Silence Sanctuary

Inner quiet is not a blank; it is a lively area brimming with possibilities. It's a place where the mind may stop racing and enable clarity and insight to emerge. This quiet is the calm that remains even in the midst of cacophony, not the absence of noise. It's the serene core around which the maelstrom of ideas, emotions, and experiences revolves.

This inner silent refuge is frequently characterized as a place of great serenity and connection. It's where you may feel connected to yourself, others, and the environment around you. You encounter your genuine self in this space—beyond roles, titles, and expectations. It's a place where you may watch your thoughts without judgment, feel your emotions without becoming overwhelmed, and tap into an inner stream of understanding.

Inner Silence: The Science of It

Meditation's advantages, notably the sense of inner quiet, are not only anecdotal. Scientific studies have shed light on the neurological alterations that occur during meditation. Regular meditation has been demonstrated in brain imaging studies to cause structural and functional changes in regions related with attention, emotional control, and self-awareness. The brain's default mode network, which is responsible for mind-wandering and self-referential thinking, becomes less active during meditation. This decreased activity is associated with less ruminating and more present-moment awareness. Meditation has also been proven to reduce the activity of the amygdala, the brain's "fight or flight" area, resulting in less reaction to stresses and improved emotional control.

The Internal Journey

Meditation is neither a fast remedy nor a goal. It's an inside journey—an investigation of the terrain of your mind, emotions, and consciousness. The depths of your awareness, like the depths of the ocean, are a huge realm waiting to be disclosed.

The path of meditation requires patience. It is about constantly turning up to the practice, regardless of whether you feel rapid breakthroughs or not. With practice and commitment, you'll discover that times of inner quiet grow more common and deep.

Meditation is a portal to the richness of inner silence—an oasis of calm in the midst of modern life's desert. It demonstrates the interconnection of all human experiences beyond cultural and geographical borders. Meditation provides the gift of self-awareness, emotional equilibrium, and the discovery of the infinite depths inside via mindfulness and quiet.

As you begin on this path, keep in mind that meditation isn't about attaining a state of permanent joy or distancing yourself from the outside world. It is about developing the ability to manage the world with more clarity and resilience. It's about realizing that the refuge of inner stillness exists inside you, waiting to be revealed by the simple act of sitting still and going within. During this journey, you may discover that the depths of your inner quiet reflect the grandeur of the cosmos, which is both mysterious and awe-inspiring, both a source of wonder and a reminder of your tremendous interconnectedness with all that exists.

CHAPTER 8. The Art of Deep Listening: Hearing the Whispers of Stillness

In a world filled with noise and constant distractions, the art of deep listening emerges as a transformative practice, allowing us to connect with the subtle rhythms of existence, hear the whispers of our own intuition, and attune ourselves to the stillness that resides within and around us. Deep listening is an act of present, a manner of connecting with the environment that fosters empathy, understanding, and a profound connection to the core of life itself.

Above and Beyond Surface Sounds

We are frequently surrounded by a symphony of noises in our hectic lives—traffic, talk, music, and the buzz of electronics. In the midst of this noise, the practice of deep listening invites us to go beyond the surface and into the core of sound. It is an invitation to transcend beyond the audible and tune into the finer aspects of vibration and resonance.

Deep listening begins with being totally present. It's about paying attention to the noises around us, whether it's the rustling of leaves, the hum of a refrigerator, or the rhythm of our own breathing. We begin to perceive layers of nuance as we get more used to these sounds—the softness within the loud, the pauses between notes, and the harmonies that weave together the fabric of auditory experience.

The Wisdom of Silence

A meeting with quiet is at the center of profound listening. This may appear contradictory, given that stillness is frequently linked with quiet. True stillness, on the other hand, is more than just the lack of sound; it is a condition of inner peace that remains independent of outward disturbance. Deep listening helps us to access this pool of calm inside ourselves, even in the midst of upheaval in the outside world.

We make room for the knowledge of quiet to emerge when we listen intently. It is in this place that insights, intuitions, and heightened awareness emerge. We build a bridge between the exterior and interior worlds by engaging with sound thoughtfully. We find serenity, understanding, and the ability to connect with the deep pool of wisdom that dwells inside us on this bridge.

Connection and Empathy

Deep listening is a strong skill for connecting with others in addition to engaging with our own internal environment. When we sincerely listen to someone, we give them a valuable gift: our full attention and presence. Empathy is shown by deep listening; it is a means of expressing, "I see you, I hear you, and I am here for you."

Deep listening is becoming increasingly rare in our fast-paced and fractured environment. We frequently engage in talks while distracted by our electronics or busy with our own ideas. We may overcome these hurdles and create true connections with people around us by practicing deep listening. We create an environment in which they may be heard, affirmed, and understood, generating a sense of connection and mutual respect.

Deep Listening as a Practice

Consider incorporating the following methods into your everyday life to build the art of deep listening:

1. Silent Moments: Set aside time each day to listen to the softer noises in your environment. Allow the distant murmur of nature, or the soft rustle of leaves, to bring you into the present now.

2. Mindful Soundscapes: Take a few moments to listen to the noises around you carefully. Begin by focusing on what's nearby—the ticking of a clock, the creaking of a chair—and gradually broaden your awareness to encompass more distant noises.

3. Listening Meditation: Close your eyes and focus your attention on the soundscape to practice listening meditation. Take note of the many levels of sound, from front to background.

Allow yourself to be completely immersed in the audio experience.

4. Empathetic Conversations: Practice active listening when having conversations. Set aside your personal agenda and focus entirely on the speaker's words. Reflect on what they're saying to guarantee comprehension and demonstrate that you're actually listening.

5. Nature Immersion: Spend time outside and immerse yourself in the sounds of nature. Nature provides a rich tapestry of sounds that may strengthen your listening practice, whether it's the chirping of birds, the rustling of leaves, or the cadence of ocean waves.

Deep listening transcends the surface levels of sound and allows us to delve into the complexities of reality. We connect with the cycles of life, expose ourselves to the knowledge of quiet, and promote empathy and connection with others by engaging with sound attentively.

Deep listening is a lifelong habit that evolves with each passing moment. When we practice deep listening, we not only improve our capacity to connect with the world around us, but we also open the door to the tremendous reservoir of knowledge and insight that exists inside us. We go on a transforming journey with this exercise, one that takes us from cacophony to silence, from distraction to presence, and from isolation to connection. Deep listening helps us to hear the whispers of silence amid the music of life and, as a result, discover a profound connection to the center of existence itself.

CHAPTER 9. Movement as Meditation: Dancing, Walking, and Yoga

Images of sitting folks in peaceful concentration typically spring to mind when we think about meditation. However, meditation is more than just sitting motionless; it is a dynamic practice that may be conveyed via movement. Movement as meditation enables us to investigate the fundamental relationship that exists between the body and the mind, providing avenues to self-discovery, awareness, and a better knowledge of the present moment. Dancing, walking, and yoga are three strong forms of movement meditation that allow us to integrate the physical and spiritual, establishing a harmonic balance of motion and calm.

Dancing: The Art of Physical Expression
Dancing is a global language, speaking to the essence of human experience and transcending cultures. Dancing as a kind of meditation helps

us to express ourselves without using words by tapping into the reservoir of emotions and experiences that exist inside our bodies. Dancing becomes a channel for self-discovery, creativity, and awareness, whether via established dance forms or spontaneous movements.

The mind and body connect in a smooth flow when dancing. You become totally absorbed in the present moment as you move to the rhythm of music or your own breath. The sensations in your body, the energy running through your limbs, and the emotions inspired by the music all come together to form a state of concentrated awareness.

Dancing as meditation allows you to let go of inhibitions and self-judgment. It is a discipline of submitting to the music and allowing your body to move freely, free of cultural rules or expectations. Dancing becomes a type of release via this freedom of expression—a method to shed the layers of ego and delve into a more real sense of self.

Walking: A Mindful Steps Journey

Walking is a commonplace action that is frequently overlooked. Walking, when handled mindfully, may become a contemplative exercise that reconnects us to our bodies, the environment, and the rhythm of life. Walking meditation entails paying close attention to each stride, fostering a profound engagement with the present moment.

Walking meditation is all about slowing down and tuning in. You become aware of the sensation of your feet making contact with the earth with each step—the pressure, movement, and small weight adjustments. This focused concentration keeps you in the current moment, keeping your mind from wandering into previous regrets or future concerns.

Walking meditation can be done inside or outside, on a calm route or a busy metropolitan street. Walking, regardless of the situation, becomes a rhythmic ballet between movement and silence. You walk in a smooth rhythm that matches the natural ebb and flow of breath, bringing your inner world into harmony with the outside world.

Yoga is a practice that unites the body, mind, and soul.

Yoga, an ancient Indian discipline, is a profound embodiment of movement as meditation. It is a comprehensive method that combines physical postures (asanas), breath control (pranayama), and meditation (dhyana). Yoga becomes a transforming journey that nurtures the body, relaxes the mind, and awakens the soul when these aspects are combined.

Yoga promotes the thoughtful examination of one's own body's potential and limits. As you go through the postures, your attention is drawn to the sensations, alignment, and breath connected with each one. This concentrated attention helps you to connect with the knowledge of your body and build a deep feeling of present.

The breath is essential in yoga, acting as a link between the physical and the mental. Pranayama techniques teach you how to control your breath, encouraging it to flow freely and regularly. This deliberate control of the breath has a tremendous influence on the mind, settling mental oscillations and ultimately to a condition of inner quiet.

Meditation practice is smoothly integrated into the fabric of movement in yoga. You have the opportunity to experience meditation in motion as you flow through asanas. Each posture becomes a time of reflection, an opportunity to turn your focus within and investigate the relationship between the body, the breath, and the mind.

Integration of Motion and Stillness

Dance, strolling, and yoga are all forms of movement, yet they also serve as portals to silence. The transitions between poses in yoga, the tiny periods of calm between steps in walking meditation, and the moments of silent surrender inside a dance all need a careful balance of motion and pause.

This fusion of movement and quiet exemplifies the linked essence of existence. It depicts the continual dance between activity and repose, progress and meditation, and action and contemplation that is life itself.

The Influence of Presence

The power of presence—the art of being totally connected with the unfolding moment—is taught to us via movement as meditation. We learn to embody awareness in action via activities such as dancing, walking, and yoga. These practices remind us that meditation is more than a cushion or a silent room; it is a way of life that encourages awareness, insight, and a profound connection to our inner selves.

Remember that the purpose of movement as meditation isn't perfection or reaching a certain result. It's about accepting the trip and letting the movement be the meditation. Approach the practice with an open heart and a responsive mind, whether you're dancing, strolling, or flowing through yoga poses. Accept the dance between movement and stillness and allow yourself to be surprised by the beauty of presence in every stride, stance, and moment of the trip.

PART V: STILLNESS AS A PATH TO TRANSFORMATION

CHAPTER 10. The Journey Inward: Discovering Your True Self through Stillness

Stillness may appear alien, even paradoxical, in a world that lives on perpetual action. Yet, it is in the depths of quiet that we discover the most fundamental truths about ourselves—the substance of our being that is frequently buried by the external demands of life. The internal journey, guided by the practice of silence, allows us to peel back the layers of identification, untangle the complexity of the mind, and eventually uncover the true core of who we actually are.

The Modern Conundrum

The speed of life in the modern day has reached new heights. Work, technology, and cultural expectations frequently drown out the subtle murmurs of our inner selves. We are trapped in a never-ending loop of doing, pursuing external affirmation, and seeking satisfaction through material pursuits.

This exterior attention might cause us to feel disconnected from our actual selves. We begin to identify with positions, labels, and accomplishments, losing sight of the greater store of wisdom inside us. The inward journey is an antidote to this quandary—a path that urges us to shift our focus from the outside world to the unexplored territory of our inner realm.

The Power of Silence
Stillness is more than just the lack of movement; it is a condition of inner quiet—a conscious halt in the midst of existence's commotion. The mind's continual chatter begins to fade in silence, and we make room for self-reflection and self-discovery. Stillness serves as a blank canvas on which the reality of our being can be revealed.

We welcome silence into our lives via disciplines such as meditation, mindfulness, and contemplation. We go on a voyage deeper into the caverns of our mind by carefully shifting our focus away from outward distractions.

Peeling Back the Layers

We meet the layers that comprise our identity when we move inside. These layers are frequently formed by cultural conventions, familial influences, prior experiences, and life conditioning. Fears, limiting beliefs, and attachments may all materialize as layers that conceal our genuine self.

Peeling back these layers one by one is part of the process of realizing your actual self. It is a process of examining embedded narratives in your mind and investigating ideas that may not fully connect with your authentic nature. It's about removing the masks you've worn to adapt to external standards and revealing your true self.

Listening to Your Inner Whispers

Stillness urges us to listen—not to the outside world, but to our own inner whispers. In the stillness, we begin to hear the voice of intuition—the intelligent, unfiltered wisdom that comes from a place beyond the clamor of the mind. Intuition frequently talks softly, and we may comprehend its messages only in silence.

Listening to the whispering within necessitates an open heart and an open intellect. It entails letting go of the ego's demand for control and allowing ourselves to be directed by our inner wisdom's deeper currents. This advice may manifest as gut sensations, intuitive insights, or a deep sense of knowing.

Increasing Self-Awareness

The internal journey is an ongoing process of developing self-awareness. Self-awareness is the foundation for knowing who you actually are. It entails monitoring your thoughts, feelings, and behaviors without making any judgments.

Self-awareness allows you to acquire insight into your behavioral patterns, triggers, and the underlying motives that drive your behaviors.

Mindfulness, a type of present-moment consciousness, fosters self-awareness. Paying attention to your ideas and feelings as they occur allows you to become acquainted with your mind's inner terrain. This technique sheds light on ideas that come without conscious effort, exposing unconscious beliefs that form your experience of yourself and the world.

Accepting Authenticity
The voyage within finally leads to authenticity. Authenticity entails accepting your genuine self, with all of its flaws and shortcomings. It entails connecting your actions with your beliefs, being honest about your thoughts and feelings, and living in accordance with your inner truth.
Authenticity necessitates bravery—the fortitude to face your fears, accept vulnerability, and step into your power. On this journey, the silence you create becomes a space where you may connect

with your inner principles and discover the route that resonates with your real self.

This path needs commitment, patience, and a willingness to explore oneself. It is not a destination to be attained; rather, it is a continuous process of increasing your relationship with yourself. The internal journey is an act of self-love—a tribute to your determination to acknowledge your genuine identity, create self-awareness, and accept the authenticity that lies at the heart of your existence.

Remember that the route may not always be clear when you begin on your adventure. There may be times of doubt and difficulty along the path. However, it is in the silence that you will discover the power, resilience, and knowledge to manage the twists and turns. The interior journey demonstrates your ability for development, transformation, and the never-ending investigation of the unfathomable depths inside you.

CHAPTER 11. Healing through Stillness: Nurturing Emotional Well-being

While the road to emotional recovery may appear complicated, stillness provides a simple yet profound approach to traverse the waves of emotions, grow self-awareness, and finally find peace and balance within oneself.

The Practice of Emotional Stillness

The practice of emotional stillness is creating a mental and emotional space in which you may observe your feelings without judgment. The goal of this technique is to create a pause—a space between the stimulation of an emotion and your reaction to it. During this time, you have the option of engaging with the feeling intentionally rather than reacting impulsively.

Find a quiet place and sit in a comfortable position to develop emotional stillness. Bring your attention to the feelings in your body while you breathe deeply. Take note of any points of tension or pain. Imagine inhaling peace and expelling stress as you concentrate on your breathing.

Now, pay attention to your feelings. Allow whatever emotion you're feeling to rise to the top of your mind. Instead of pushing it away or feeling overwhelmed by it, watch it objectively. Take note of any bodily symptoms linked with the emotion, such as chest tightness, stomach fluttering, or a sense of burning.

As you continue to examine the experience, tell yourself that it is normal to feel the way you do. Avoid assigning labels or making judgments about the emotion. Instead, merely accept its presence and let it be without attempting to change it. You're building a container for the feeling to be acknowledged and expressed in this area of silence.

Getting Rid of Emotional Baggage

Emotional stillness may be used to release emotional baggage, which is the accumulation of unprocessed feelings that can weigh you down.

You give yourself the chance to address, analyze, and release these emotions in a healthy and beneficial way by practicing stillness.

Suppressed emotions frequently persist in the subconscious mind, impacting your ideas, behaviors, and interactions without your conscious knowledge. By shining a light of awareness on these emotions, you bring them to the surface, where they may be recognized, felt, and finally let go.

Embracing Mindfulness

The practice of mindfulness—being completely present in the moment—serves as a guiding concept throughout the journey of emotional healing via quiet. Mindfulness enables you to examine your thoughts and emotions without being caught up in them. This nonjudgmental awareness bridges the gap between stimulus and response, allowing you to choose how you respond to your emotions.

You grow more able to regulate the ebb and flow of emotions as you build awareness via the practice of emotional quiet. You reply with aim and awareness rather than impulsively. This transition from reaction to response gives you the ability to interact with your emotions in a way that promotes healing and emotional well-being.

Creating Inner Space
Stillness practice provides inner space—the spaciousness in which emotions can flow without becoming overpowering. You acquire perspective on your emotions in this area, realizing that they are fleeting sensations that come and go. This knowledge frees you from the grasp of overwhelming emotions, allowing you to approach them with greater calm.

Creating inner space entails distancing yourself from the emotional narratives. Instead of getting caught up in the stories your mind creates, you observe your emotions as energy moving through your body. This adjustment in perspective keeps you from falling into rumination or exaggerating the severity of your emotions.

Healing as a Process

Emotional healing via quiet is a journey that takes time to complete. This journey must be approached with patience and self-compassion. Emotional wounds, like physical wounds, require caring and care to heal.

There may be times when you find resistance, when particular feelings feel overwhelming, or when the healing process appears to be taking a long time. During these times, remind yourself that recovery is not a straight line. It's about making small steps forward, seeing failures as chances for growth, and treating yourself with love every step of the way.

The path to healing via silence invites you to be present with your emotions, to hold space for them, and to create a profound sense of self-awareness and self-compassion. You learn to traverse the complicated landscape of emotions with more ease and resilience by practicing emotional stillness. You establish a safe haven in which to face, process, and release emotional baggage, promoting deep healing and emotional well-being.

Remember that you are not alone as you begin on this path. Stillness is a timeless technique that has been adopted by civilizations and wisdom systems throughout history. You are giving yourself a gift by adding emotional quiet into your everyday life—a gift of self-discovery, emotional emancipation, and the ability to nurture your own emotional well-being.

CHAPTER 12. From Chaos to Clarity: Finding Answers in the Stillness Within

Finding solutions to life's questions might feel like traveling through a murky fog in our fast-paced and loud environment. Despite the turmoil of outward stimuli and incessant distractions, there remains a sanctuary—a place of calm within us—where clarity and insights await. The route from chaos to clarity is a transforming one, driven by the discipline of finding answers in the profound quiet that exists at our center.

The Quest for Answers

Life is full of questions—questions about our purpose, decisions, relationships, and the path we should pursue. In our search for solutions, we frequently explore external sources, seek counsel from others, or depend on our analytical brains. While these tactics might be beneficial, they can also add to the cacophony, trapping us more in the complexities of our inquiry.

However, the solutions we seek are not necessarily available in the outside world. True wisdom is often found within us—in the depths of our awareness, where our intuition, inner knowing, and intrinsic wisdom exist. The path from chaos to clarity challenges us to delve within, to tap into the calm within in order to uncover the solutions that are particularly suited to our specific journey.

Developing the Question
The path from chaos to clarity starts with nurturing the inquiry itself. We are frequently so intent on obtaining the answer that we fail to thoroughly phrase the inquiry. A well-phrased inquiry serves as a compass, directing our attention and purpose toward the answers we seek.

Create your inquiry with purpose and detail. Rather than asking, "What should I do?"

consider, "What step can I take to align with my purpose?"

Getting into the Inner Sanctuary

You're ready to enter the inner sanctuary of quiet after you've nurtured your query. Locate a peaceful and comfortable location where you will not be disturbed. To center yourself, sit in a comfortable posture, close your eyes, and take a few deep breaths.

Bring your query to the forefront of your thoughts while you shift your attention within. Hold the question lightly, without expecting a fast response. Allow the question to sink into your mind before releasing any connection to finding an immediate response.

The Dance of Patience and Receptivity

The path from chaos to clarity is a dance of patience and openness. It's about letting the solutions come to you organically, rather than forcing or speeding the process. Thoughts, ideas, or sensations may arise while you sit in silence with your inquiry. These are your inner wisdom's whispers.

Be open to whatever comes your way. It may not always take the form of explicit words or straightforward responses. It might take the form of a mood, a vision, an experience, or an intuitive understanding. Believe in your ability to discern the truth as it emerges inside you.

Embracing the Unknown
The answers you seek in the domain of silence may not necessarily be the ones you expect. The road from chaos to clarity might sometimes lead to the revelation that you don't have all the answers—and that's completely fine. The process of seeking answers inside is about facing the uncertainty with bravery and an open heart, not seeking certainties.

Stillness challenges us to let go of our demand for quick fixes and to trust in the unfolding of life's mysteries. Clarity is typically revealed gradually, rather than as a single conclusive answer—a growing sense of comprehension, an inner knowing, or a novel viewpoint that lights the route ahead.

Integration and Action

The road from chaos to clarity does not end with quiet; it continues into action. Carry the insights and knowledge you've gained from your contemplative practice into your daily life when you emerge from your practice. Consider how the answers you've discovered might influence your future decisions, interactions, and choices.

Sometimes the solution is not a precise action, but a movement in perspective—a transformation in how you approach difficulties, make decisions, or interpret your situation. The genuine value of the answers you find in stillness is their capacity to direct you toward better harmony with your authentic self and your particular journey.

The path from chaos to clarity—from perplexity to insight—is proof of the transformational power of silence. We discover answers that resonate with the deepest elements of our being in the refuge of silence inside. This voyage serves as a reminder that, among the chaos and complexities of life, there is a fountain of knowledge just waiting to be discovered.

Remember that the route from chaos to clarity is not linear as you traverse the twists and turns of your own trip. It's a never-ending cycle of searching, discovering, and receiving. You go on a journey that recognizes your unique path and helps you to handle life's problems with a fresh sense of clarity and purpose by cultivating quiet, developing meaningful questions, and appreciating the wisdom that comes.

CONCLUSION: Embracing Stillness as a Lifelong Companion

We've looked at how stillness can improve our lives in a variety of ways, from finding inner calm in the midst of chaos to fostering emotional well-being, discovering our actual selves, and seeking answers inside.

Embracing stillness is a lifetime path that urges us to return to the source of serenity inside ourselves on a regular basis. As we get to the end of our journey, consider the essence of silence as a lifelong friend.

The Constant Sanctuary

Life's difficulties, uncertainties, and pressures are unavoidable. Still, in the middle of these events, quiet serves as a sanctuary—a safe haven to which we may always return. It is a location where we may escape the commotion of the outside world and reconnect with the serenity within ourselves.

Stillness is a continuous friend no matter where we go in life. Whether we're celebrating a wonderful occasion or facing misfortune, the practice of stillness provides an anchor—a place where we may center ourselves, regroup, and find clarity among the tumult.

A Self-Discovery Path

The quest for self-discovery is a lifetime endeavor, an adventure that leads us through numerous stages, each exposing fresh aspects of our genuine selves. In this journey, stillness is a useful guide, allowing us to discover truths that resonate with our basic nature.

We create a place for introspection and self-reflection when we calm the mind and enjoy the vastness of silence. We learn to listen to our intuition's whispers, to accept our vulnerabilities, and to abandon the masks we've worn to comply to conventional standards. We emerge from this process as more honest and powerful versions of ourselves.

Accepting the Process

The goal of stillness practice is not to achieve everlasting tranquility or to silence the mind eternally. It's about accepting the process—the ups and downs of thinking, the periods of clarity and unrest. The path of stillness, like the journey of existence, is a dynamic one.
There may be moments when the mind is especially busy or when quiet is unattainable. These are not failures, but rather chances for progress. tolerating silence as a lifetime friend entails tolerating mental changes with tolerance and without judgment.

A Gateway to Presence
In a world that frequently pulls us in a thousand different directions, the practice of stillness is a window to presence—a portal to the richness of the present moment. We learn to build present in our interactions, experiences, and everyday routines via stillness.

The practice of stillness helps us to fully immerse ourselves in the here and now, whether we're relishing a cup of tea, engaging in conversation, or simply watching the world around us. This presence enhances our experiences, strengthens our connections, and adds a sense of wonder to every moment.

Developing Gratitude

Accepting silence as a lifetime companion urges us to practice gratitude—for the gift of quiet as well as the insights, tranquility, and transformation it offers to our lives. Gratitude becomes a thread that runs through our path, reminding us to value the practice of quiet and all the ways it enhances our lives.

Finally, stillness is a way of being—a method of engaging with life that promotes self-awareness, emotional well-being, and a profound connection to our real selves. May we continue to accept silence as a lifetime companion—a consistent source of knowledge, peace, and progress on the ever-changing road of self-discovery and self-mastery.

www.ingramcontent.com/pod-product-compliance
Lightning Source LLC
Chambersburg PA
CBHW061004260726

48661CB00005B/2048